José Iesca Rodrigues
Ana Carolina Freixa Matsushige
Edineide Maria de Oliveira

# Business Intelligence

**José Iesca Rodrigues**
**Ana Carolina Freixa Matsushige**
**Edineide Maria de Oliveira**

# Business Intelligence

## The use of Business Intelligence - BI tools in companies

**ScienciaScripts**

**Imprint**
Any brand names and product names mentioned in this book are subject to trademark, brand or patent protection and are trademarks or registered trademarks of their respective holders. The use of brand names, product names, common names, trade names, product descriptions etc. even without a particular marking in this work is in no way to be construed to mean that such names may be regarded as unrestricted in respect of trademark and brand protection legislation and could thus be used by anyone.

Cover image: www.ingimage.com

This book is a translation from the original published under ISBN 978-620-6-75988-1.

Publisher:
Sciencia Scripts
is a trademark of
Dodo Books Indian Ocean Ltd. and OmniScriptum S.R.L publishing group

120 High Road, East Finchley, London, N2 9ED, United Kingdom
Str. Armeneasca 28/1, office 1, Chisinau MD-2012, Republic of Moldova, Europe
Printed at: see last page
**ISBN: 978-620-8-18693-7**

# Table of contents

# Introduction

The 2020 pandemic has accelerated digital transformation in all sectors of the economy. As a result, the volume of data created and stored has grown exponentially, making digital a reality in any organization. According to Exame magazine (2021), 40 trillion gigabytes of digital data were generated worldwide in 2020.

According to research by Chen, Chang and Storey (2012, pg. 1165-1188), an evolution of BI is in the 3.0 model, in which the key points occur through content generated by sensors and cell phones. These provide: person-centered analysis, location analysis, analysis pertinent to the context and, finally, human-computer interaction (HCI). Every day, thousands of bytes of data are generated from social media posts, apps, photo and video uploads, smartphone signals, credit card records, browsing and sensors of various kinds.

Thus, according to Eduardo Magrani (2018, p. 44), the phenomenon that best represents the above is the so-called Internet of Things (IoT). This expression is used to describe the connectivity and interaction between various types of everyday objects that are sensitive to the internet. For example, Amazon Alexas, household appliances, light bulbs, etc. It therefore refers to a world where objects and people, as well as data and virtual environments, interact with each other in the same time and space.

Also, according to Magrani (2018, pg. 76 - 77), the Brazilian business community has already realized the potential of the Internet of Things (IoT). In a survey carried out by Accenture (2015), Brazilian interviewees revealed that they were aware of the opportunities that the IoT can offer. In addition, they highlighted the three main expected benefits: increased employee productivity, cost cutting and optimized use of their assets.

However, this huge supply of data demands that analysis be more precise and that the choice of indicators for these evaluations be accurate. In addition, the business environment is constantly evolving, becoming increasingly complex and competitive, requiring organizations to update and make their decision-making process more agile, strategic and tactical.

This is when *Business Intelligence* is used, the main objective of which is to provide interactive access to data, enabling it to be manipulated and offering both managers and analysts the ability to conduct analysis. This facilitates the process of making more informed and, consequently, more assertive management decisions.

In addition, data analysis is widely used in day-to-day business and is sometimes confused with BI. According to the Institute for Operations Research and Management Science (2022), Informs, it represents the combination of computerized technology, management science techniques and statistics to solve real problems.

Today, knowledge is extremely valuable to organizations all over the world. Consequently, the sheer volume of disconnected information in various formats represents one of the first obstacles to data analysis and business intelligence.

It is also important to emphasize the need to implement strategic planning in companies seeking growth and development. Strategic management is characterized by the way in which an organization's resources are managed, with the aim of achieving results and goals that make the business more effective.

We can therefore say that aligning data analysis with strategic management allows the company to base itself on both data and results, directing its actions towards a more assertive path. Data analysis allows the company to draw up a strategic plan with greater certainty, understanding what the organization's opportunities and challenges are.

The ultimate aim of this work is to find out the main benefit and how Business Intelligence tools, such as Power BI, are used in companies operating in various sectors. Based on the analysis of aspects such as decision-making, strategic management and competitive advantage. The intermediate objectives are: to analyze the impact of Power BI on making more assertive decisions, to understand the tool's impact on developing competitive advantages, to study strategic management and to recognize the importance of the *Business Intelligence* area in an organization.

In 2022, the Gartner Group carried out a survey that separated Business Intelligence tools and Analytics Platforms into four quadrants: challengers, leaders, visionaries and niche. In this study, Power BI was categorized as a leader, ahead of tools such as Tableau, Qlikview and Google Data Studio.

According to Martins (2016, p. 12), "no matter how complex the systems, no one makes decisions without data, that is, the persistence, reliability and integrity of information are key to predictive analysis, so that, based on past data, the future is analyzed and projected."

According to Braghittoni (2017, pg. 29), initially, the implementation of Business Intelligence tools usually takes place in a particular area, which understands the need for it and seeks to implement it. Usually, in the beginning, this pioneering area in the company will be alone in this endeavor, which demonstrates the need for easy-to-use tools.

In order to be able to analyze the strategic effect of Power BI on companies, it is necessary to know some technical concepts such as: *Business Intelligence*, Data Analysis and the tools used in this process, such as Power BI. You also need to understand the decision-making process and strategic management. In order to be able to use this information to understand the positive consequences of using these tools in organizations.

We will cover the following subjects for a better understanding of this study: what is *Business Intelligence* ; the use of data analysis; what methods and tools are used; what is Power BI and what are its competitors; the importance of strategic management; the use of BI tools to support the decision-making process; and, finally, the use of *Business Intelligence* to gain competitive advantage.

## Chapter 1 - Business Intelligence - BI

The term *Business Intelligence* first appeared in 1865, used by Richard Millar Devens to tell the story of banker Sir Henry Fernese, who made a huge profit based on information obtained directly from his environment and his competitors.

> "He who knows the enemy and himself will fight a hundred battles without losing; for him who does not know the enemy but knows himself, the chances for victory or defeat will be equal; he who knows neither the enemy nor himself will be defeated in every battle." (TZU. Art of War, 2019) (TZU, Sun. The Art of War, 2019)

Today, a good BI system contains all the information that executives need. Its main objective is to make it possible to access data interactively, often in real time. Consequently, it helps to develop appropriate analyses of the business.

Therefore, according to Mengwei Lu (2014, pg. 12), BI aims to "help the company extract useful information from all internal and external data sources efficiently and effectively, in order to make it available to decision-makers at any time and from anywhere, when needed". It is therefore possible to generate *insights*, which result in assertive decision-making; more effective operations and business processes; and increased competitive advantages.

In addition, for Palge Batzan (2016, pg. 11), "first-line managers use *BI* to define the future of the business, analyze markets, industries and economies in order to determine the strategic direction the company must follow to remain profitable."

A survey carried out by Forbes Insights (2016, pg. 6), reported that organizations that invest in *Business Intelligence* are achieving groundbreaking returns. Thus, the success of Business Intelligence programs generates substantial tangible and intangible benefits for companies.

Consequently, according to research by Forbes (2016, pg. 6), as we can see in Figure 1, the benefits cover a wide range of organizational activities and processes, including: improved customer metrics; accelerated time to market; an increasingly strong portfolio of products and services; brand appreciation and recognition, generating greater profitability.

Figure 1: Where BI causes results.

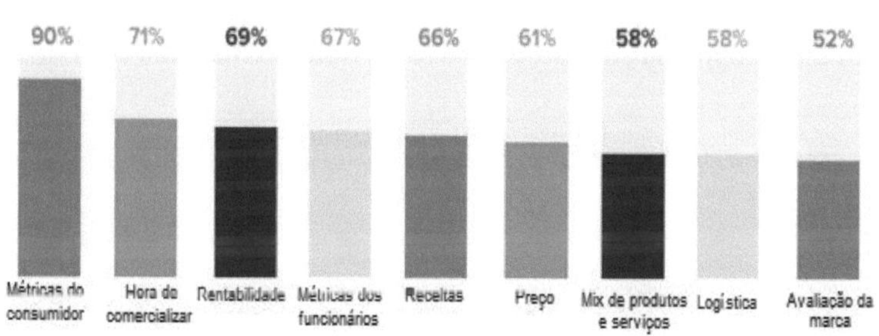


Source: Adapted from Forbes Insights - 2016, pg. 6

In view of what was demonstrated by the research carried out by Forbes Insights (2016, pg. 6), "*Breakthrough Business Intelligence*", we can understand that the use of Business Intelligence and BI tools generates several benefits for organizations. Thus, allowing companies to have greater control over their data, resulting in increased revenue and profitability.

According to Francisco Neto (2014, pg. 36), BI tools are capable of displaying a set of data through the use of summaries, dashboards, reports, graphs and maps. Consequently, for him, this is justified by the fact that *Business Intelligence* brings information together in one place.

Thus, according to author Ramesh Sharda (2019, pg. 16), a Business Intelligence model has four main components: the *Data Warehouse* (DW), used to store data in an organized way (database); business analysis, which aims to manipulate, mine and analyze this information taken from the DW; BPM, which monitors and analyzes performance; and finally, the user interface (dashboard), which allows managers to visualize this data.

We can see in the following image, Figure 2, proposed by W. Eckerson (2003, pg. 32), taken from the book Smart Companies in the 21st Century: The Secrets of Creating Successful Business Intelligent Solutions, the relationship between the components described above by Ramesh Sharda.

Figure 2: BI architecture.

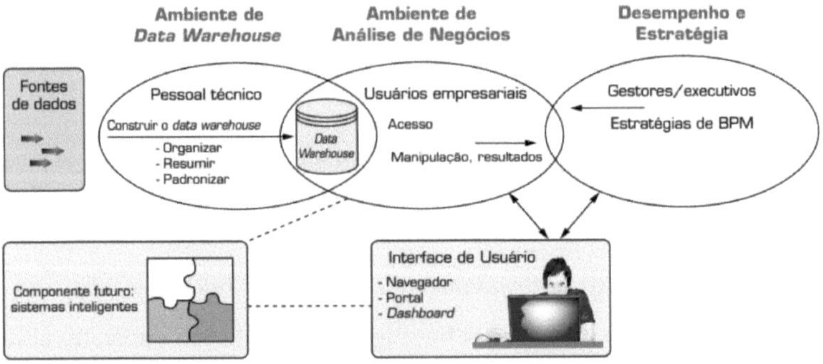

Source: W. Eckerson, Smart Companies in the 21st Century: The Secrets of Creating Successful Business Intelligent Solutions. The Data Warehousing Institute, Seattle, WA, 2003, p. 32, Illustration 5.

# Chapter 2 - Data Analysis Applied to Business

Research by the International Data Corporation (IDC) (2020) has shown that the amount of data created and replicated has increased significantly. According to them, this is due to the growth in the number of people working, studying and having fun directly from their homes due to the pandemic.

According to author Ramesh Sharda (2019, pg. 23), "data analysis can be seen as the process of developing decisions or practical recommendations for action based on glimpses generated by historical data". Therefore, when applied to business, data analysis has as its main objectives the development of reports that demonstrate the current and future results of the organization, so that the administrator can then make assertive and strategic decisions.

According to a study carried out by the IDC consultancy (2020), Brazilian companies that invested in data analysis in order to improve their decision-making process saw an average increase in revenue of 21%. In addition, the research showed that there were increases of around 16% in operational efficiency, 20% in profit generated and 24% in employee retention.

Thus, in view of the above, we can understand the importance of data analysis in companies' results, directly impacting on their efficiency, revenue, profit and the retention of qualified employees. Consequently, it increases their competitive advantage over other companies.

According to the *Institute for Operations Research and Management Science (Informs)* (*"What are Operations Research and Analytics?"*, 2022), data analysis has three levels, as we can see in the following image (Figure 3): the descriptive level, which aims to define problems and opportunities; the predictive level, which seeks to make accurate projections of future results and events; and finally, the prescriptive level, which defines the best actions and decisions to be taken.

Figure 3: The three types of data analysis.

Source: Sharda, 2019 pg. 24.

# Chapter 3 - Methods and Tools Used in BI

According to an article written by Doug Dailey of IBM (2019) "BI platforms must have dashboard creation, on-demand report creation and data visualization capabilities". Considering this, the company cited the three main components of Business Intelligence software, which are: *Data Warehouse* (DW), ETL and OLAP.

Thus, according to them, the DW is intended to be a central data repository that supports business analysis and reporting tools (such as Power BI). In the case of ETL, *Extract Transform Load*, the component is responsible for combining data from multiple sources, consisting of three stages: extraction, transformation and loading.

Finally, the OLAP tool, *On-Line Analytical* Processing, performs online analytical processing, reorganizing the data and enabling rapid processing and analysis of data based on *insights*. The following figure, Figure 3, shows the flow of these components.

Figure 4: Three main components of BI software.

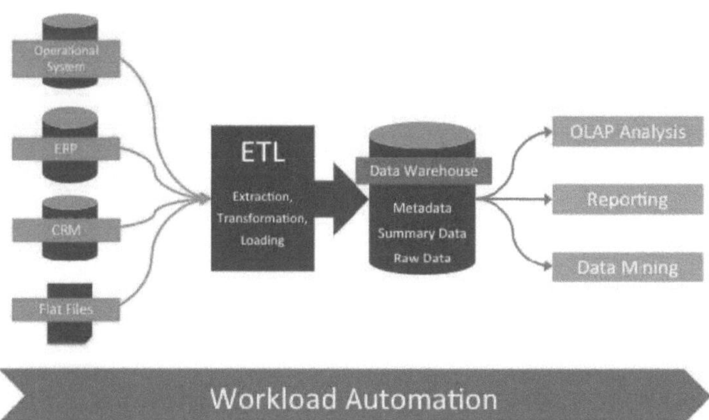

Source: ETL for OLAP

The increased need for *Business Intelligence* systems has led to a number of suppliers appearing on the technology market. However, most of the solutions they offered depended on a high level of knowledge in Information Technology, which became a problem for most users.

In addition to the above, there is the high cost of implementing the solutions offered by companies, which consequently leads to consumer dissatisfaction. Thus, the need arose for tools that are easy to manipulate, as users need to extract data and create analyses according to their needs (Mengwei Lu, 2014, pg. 2). One of the solutions to this problem was Power BI, the main tool studied in this book.

# Chapter 4 - Microsoft Power B I

Power BI (PBI) is a solution developed by Microsoft that allows users to visualize their data and share it with their organizations, and even integrate it into their websites or applications. The tool makes it possible to develop reports and dashboards without the need for specialized IT staff.

PBI was launched in 2015. According to Microsoft (2018, "Interactive learning in Microsoft Power BI."), Power BI *Desktop* has versions for Windows operating systems only, and it receives updates on a monthly basis, some of which come from comments and suggestions from users of the tool.

According to the company, Power BI is "robust and enterprise-grade, ready for extensive real-time modeling and analysis, as well as custom development". In addition, for Microsoft, it can serve as a "decision-making and analysis engine behind group projects, divisions or entire companies" (2018, "Interactive learning from Microsoft Power BI.").

According to Mengwei Lu (2014, p. 2), it is characterized as a Self-Service BI solution, and is therefore used to meet the interests of the end user. According to Cunha (2017, p. 6), "PBI is a cloud-based Self-Service BI solution, which enables data to be updated in real time. With its use, it is possible for people who do not have specific technical programming knowledge to create reports."

## 4.1 Power B competitors I

There are several tools focused on Business Intelligence. An analysis carried out by the Gartner Group in 2022 ("*Gartner Magic Quadrant for Business*

*Intelligence and Analytics Platforms*"), drew up a "magic quadrant" separating the platforms into the following quadrants: challengers, leaders, visionaries and niche.

As we can see in the following image, according to the company, the four main BI tools currently available on the market are Microsoft's Power BI, Salesforce's Tableau, Google's Google Data Studio and Qlik's Qlikview. Furthermore, by analyzing the figure below, we can conclude that Microsoft's Power BI tool was characterized as the main leader in this segment, followed by Salesforce's Tableau.

Figure 5: Magic Quadrant of Business Intelligence platforms.

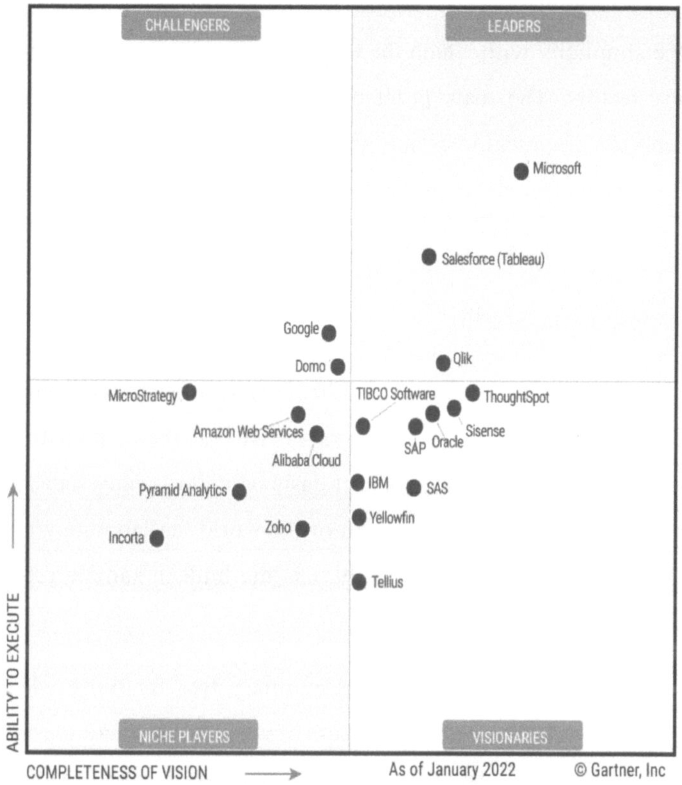

Source: Gartner Group, 2022

### 4.1.1 Tableau

One of Power BI's main competitors is Tableau, a tool developed in 2003 by students in the Computer Science department at Stanford University in the United States. According to the brand's website, the main purpose of creating this tool was to improve the flow of analysis and make data more accessible through visualization.

Due to the simplicity with which the tool is used, it is a hit with companies in various sectors. The main point of this technology is its almost total interaction via a graphical interface, and the use of *drang and drop* as a way of bringing the analyst closer to the data.

### 4.1.2 Google Data Studio

Google Data Studio was launched in 2016 by Google. According to the brand's website, the platform allows users to: visualize their data with highly configurable graphs and tables; connect dashboards to various data sources with ease; share insights with the team or the world; collaborate with their team in generating reports; and finally, use the built-in sample reports to speed up the process of creating them.

The tool's main advantage is that it is currently free for those who have emails on the Google platform. Regardless of whether the email is corporate or personal, the user can manipulate and publish the data online. On the other hand, the software is not updated as often as Power BI.

### 4.1.3 Qlikview

QlikTech is a company founded in Sweden. The tool was developed by a group of physicists who provided technology services for Tetrapak. According to the company, the software "has changed the way people use data, with intuitive visual discovery that makes business intelligence more accessible than ever".

However, the platform has two negative points: the high cost, when it becomes necessary to share the dashboards so that other users can view the data; and the need for a reasonable knowledge of IT to use the software.

## Chapter 5 - Strategic Management

The word *stratego,* from the Greek, means "general". Thus, historically, the study of strategies is based on military concepts whose main objective was to defeat enemies. After the Second World War, companies began to establish strategies similar to those used at the time in order to win the battle for the market.

However, in the business concept, not only competition and victory against the enemy were analyzed, but also the quest to achieve a desired future situation. To do this, organizations must analyse the following factors: the resources available to the company and the opportunities offered by the market.

Thus, according to Ohmae (1983, p. 36), "Without competitors there would be no need for strategy, since the sole purpose of strategic planning is to enable the company to gain, as efficiently as possible, a sustainable advantage over its competitors"

According to Oliveira (2013, pg. 4), "Administration is a structured and intuitive system that consolidates a set of principles, norms and functions to harmoniously leverage the process of planning desired future situations and their subsequent control of efficiency and productivity, as well as the organization and direction of business resources towards the expected results, with the minimization of interpersonal conflicts."

Thus, according to the author Ansoff (1993, "Implementing Strategic Management"), the main aspect of Strategic Management is related to the idea of mapping the future directions of the organization based on the resources it has. According to Pena (2018, pg. 16), strategy is:

> "(1) is a coherent, unified and integrative pattern of decisions; (2) that determines and reveals the organizational purposes in terms of its long-term objectives, action programs, and priorities for resource allocation; (3) selects the businesses in which the organization is or will be; (4) seeks to achieve a long-term sustainable advantage in each of the businesses, through appropriate responses to the opportunities and threats of the environment, and to the strengths and weaknesses of the organization; (5) encompasses all levels of the organization (corporate, business and functional); and (6) defines the nature of economic and non-economic contributions to stakeholders." (PORTER apud PENA, 2018, pg.16)

For Certo (1993, "Administração Estratégica: planejamento e implementação da estratégia"), strategic management can be defined as a continuous and interactive process that aims to keep the organization as a whole integrated with its environment in an appropriate way.

In this way, Oliveira (1991, "Estratégia empresarial: uma abordagem empreendedora") defines strategic management as the establishment of certain measures to be taken by the manager so that, in the future, the organization will have a different situation from the one it had in the past.

According to Richard Whittington (2004, "What is strategy?"), the field of Strategic Management can be defined from four generic perspectives: the classical, the processual, the evolutionary and, finally, the systematic perspective.

Thus, as we can see in figures 6 and 7, taken from the book Administração Estratégica by the author Márcio Abdala (2019, pg. 7 - 9), the approaches are conceived from the intersection of two axes: results, which presents profit maximization on the one hand and more plural results on the other; and processes, in which we can see at one end those that are deliberate and, at the other, those that are emerging.

Figure 6: Strategy quadrants,

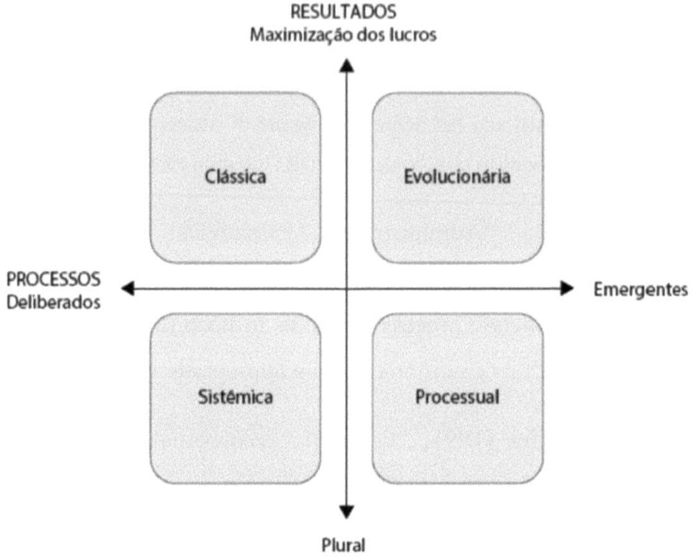

Source: Abdala, Márcio M. Strategic Administration . Available at: My Library, GEN Group, 2019.

Figure 7: Table - Strategy quadrants.

| | Clássica | Processual | Evolucionária | Sistêmica |
|---|---|---|---|---|
| **Estratégia** | Formal | Elaborada | Eficiente | Inserida |
| **Justificativa** | Maximização do lucro | Vaga | Sobrevivência | Local |
| **Foco** | Interna (planos) | Interna (política/cognições) | Externa (mercados) | Externa (sociedade) |
| **Processos** | Analítica | Negociação/ Aprendizagem | Darwiniana | Social |
| **Influências-chave** | Economia/ militarismo | Psicologia | Economia/ Biologia | Sociologia |
| **Autores-chave** | Chandler[12] Ansoff[13] Porter[14,15] | Mintzberg[5,28] Pettigrew[29] | Hannan e Freeman[27] | Granovetter[30] |
| **Surgimento** | 1960 | 1970 | 1980 | 1990 |

Source: Abdala, Márcio M. Administração Estratégica. Available at: My Library, GEN Group, 2019.

We can see that the main importance of strategic management in a company is for the organization to achieve its objectives in the future. As a result, it will make greater profits and have a strong competitive advantage over other companies in the market.

## 5.1 The importance of Strategic Management for a company

As we have seen, strategy is considered a decisive factor in organizations. It is therefore very important for companies and managers to devote a good deal of time to adapting, drawing up and reformulating their strategies.

According to the authors Bruno Fernandes and Henrique Berton (2017, pg. 15), some of the main uses of strategic management are: taking control of the organization's destiny, establishing means of control so that the company achieves its goals; seeing opportunities, looking beyond operational activities ("What's happening in the market?"); transforming threats into opportunities, through the use of promising initiatives and monitoring advances in the way of doing business; defining new directions for the organization, breaking the inertia of repeating itself in the way it does business."); transforming threats into opportunities by using promising initiatives and keeping up with advances in technology; defining new directions for the organization, breaking the inertia of repeating the way of doing business; thinking in the long term; developing an educational process and encouraging interaction and negotiation; mobilizing resources towards a common goal, unifying efforts; and, finally, promoting change.

Furthermore, according to the author Djalma Oliveira (2013, pg. 11-14), Strategic Management makes it possible to adopt increasingly simple, flexible and sustainable management models; to identify the skills of professionals; to consolidate an attitude of action geared towards the needs and expectations of the market; to improve levels of productivity, commitment, motivation and quality; and to improve company results.

## 5.2 Use of BI in Corporate Strategy Management

In this way, it becomes possible to relate the main uses of *Business Intelligence* and, consequently, *Power BI*, to Strategic Management, which has been studied in this chapter.

The main objective of BI is to provide secure and consolidated information about the organization. In this way, it allows managers to define the company's future by analyzing businesses, industries, economies and markets.

> "Managers will be able to access information "quickly" and will be able to shorten response times, thus improving decision-making processes. In this way, information will be the company's true capital, providing knowledge for immediate decisions and for those to come in the future." (PRIMAK, 2008, p.33)

While, according to author Djalma Oliveira (2013, pg. 6), "Strategic management is a management of the future that, in a structured, systemic and intuitive way, consolidates a set of principles, rules and functions to harmoniously leverage the process of planning the desired future situation of the company as a whole..."

Thus, the use of BI allows the company to use data to consolidate and base the necessary information on when planning the future situation it wants. As a result, Strategic Management becomes more assertive.

## Chapter 6 - Strategic Decision Making

Decision-making is something we do very often, so we often don't realize that we're deciding something. Every day we make different types of decisions, from those that are considered simple, with trivial consequences, to those of great complexity, which take our breath away.

According to Maçães (2018, ch. 2 - pg. 1), "Every day, managers are forced to make decisions. Whenever they perform their duties, that is, every time they plan, organize, direct or control, they are making a series of decisions, so much so that it can even be said that the main function of managers is decision-making."

According to the authors Bruno Fernandes and Henrique Berton (2017, pg. 6), in the day-to-day life of an organization, the use of the word strategy is related to making major decisions (by the company's management group). Thus, strategic decisions are characterized by having a strong long-term influence and by impacting the organization as a whole.

According to the authors, strategic decisions are made up of tactical decisions, which are at a managerial level and consist of operationalizing major strategic decisions; and operational decisions, which represent the materialization of strategic and tactical decisions (day-to-day and with a short-term impact).

Figure 8: The three levels of decision-making.

Source: Administração Estratégica - Bruno Henrique Rocha Fernandes - 2nd edition - Editora Saraiva.

A decision needs to be made when we are faced with a problem that has more than one alternative solution, thus requiring the manager to make a choice. It is important that managers know how to make decisions assertively and, as a result, reduce the risks and the possibility of choosing an ineffective option.

Thus, according to Gomes (2007, p. 18), scholars of Decision Theory have determined a process that must be followed to generate a "good decision". This process consists of twelve stages, which will be described below:

(1) "Make sure you're trying to solve the real problem;
(2) Thinking sufficiently about the problem, without taking emotional involvement into account;
(3) Get all the relevant information;
(4) Clearly identify what really matters;
(5) Explicitly consider ethical and moral commitments;
(6) Generate the widest possible set of viable alternatives;
(7) List the quantitative and qualitative objectives of decision-making;
(8) Explain the decision criteria for each objective listed;
(9) List the consequences of each alternative for each defined decision criterion;

(10) Feed back on the previous stages through analytical methods, generating new alternatives or new criteria not previously thought of;

(11) Criticize the results obtained in the previous stage;

(12) Produce clear recommendations for decision-makers."

(GOMES, 2007 apud CANARY, 2013, p.18)

According to the author Maçães (2018, chapter 2), decision-making is a rational process and not a simple act of choosing between two or more alternatives. Consequently, for him, the decision-making process consists of 8 factors that together lead to success in the decision-making process.

Figure 9: Rational Decision-Making Model.

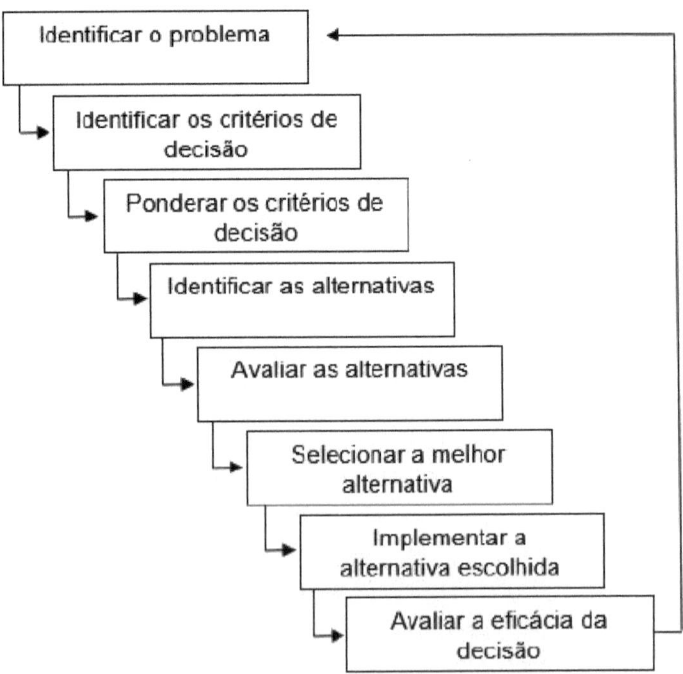

Source: Maçães, Manuel Alberto R. Planeamento, Estratégia e Tomada de Decisão - Vol. IV. Available at: Minha Biblioteca, Grupo Almedina (Portugal), 2018.

Thus, the first factor is the identification of the problem, recognizing that there is a discrepancy between the current state and the desired one. The second is represented by the identification of decision criteria, i.e. the manager must determine what is relevant when making a decision.

The third factor described by Maçães (2018) is the weighting of the decision criteria determined in the previous item. Then, in the fourth factor, it is necessary to identify the alternatives, developing and identifying viable solutions. Furthermore, the analysis of alternatives (fifth factor) aims to study the options offered by the previous stage.

Finally, the last three factors defined by the author are: the selection of the best alternative, after the analysis carried out in the previous topics; the implementation of the chosen alternative, since the decision can fail if the implementation is not adequate; and, to conclude, the evaluation of the results and effectiveness of the decision, studying the effects achieved.

## 6.1 Making decisions based on data

According to the author Neto (2020, pg. 25), "When we refer to a quality decision, we are talking about one that can be well-founded and well-justified". In the day-to-day running of organizations, the lower the risk of failure, the greater the chance of success.

Thus, according to Neto (2020), "well-founded decisions, based on information, lead us to a situation of predictability and probability of what will happen, thus allowing risk management to be carried out". Therefore, the greater the use of data, the lower the risk and, consequently, the better the decision made by the manager.

A global survey carried out by Harvard Business Review Analytic Services (HBRAS) in 2012, in which 646 executives were interviewed, revealed an evolution in the decision-making process and in the use of *Business Intelligence* and analysis tools. According to the study, this evolution is the result of four factors: improving skills, balancing data with instincts, forging new relationships and developing best practices.

Therefore, according to Cruz (2007, pg. 26-35), decision-making based on data does not entirely exclude human abilities, such as instincts, but rather complements their weaknesses. Thus, we can conclude that both data and *insights* from Business Intelligence help to make better and faster decisions in a manager's day-to-day life.

In conclusion, for Vianna and Dutra (2016, pg. 3), organizations that "are preparing for real-time decision-making based on the information collected within a large volume of generated data, will have a 20% competitive advantage over their competitors".

## Chapter 7 - Competitive Advantage

According to Bateman and Snell (1998), competitive advantages must be based on the following aspects: costs, quality, practicality, speed and innovation. They also believe that the use of planning aimed at achieving good results should be carried out in a clear, systematic and conscious way, with a view to making the right decisions that are goal-oriented.

According to Porter (1989, p.10), there are only two types of competitive advantage: low cost and differentiation. Thus, when combined with scope, the types of advantage result in three generic strategies that enable superior performance to be achieved.

As such, the author characterizes the three strategies as: cost leadership, which aims to obtain a competitive advantage by offering products and services at lower costs than the competition; differentiation, which is done by introducing one or more differentiating elements into products and services (exclusive, with higher quality or performance); and finally, focus, which seeks to focus on cost leadership, differentiation or both in a more restricted market.

Figure 101Porter's three generic strategies.

| | Custo mais baixo | Diferenciação |
|---|---|---|
| Alvo amplo | 1. Liderança no custo | 2. Diferenciação |
| | 3. (A) Enfoque no custo | 3. (B) Enfoque na diferenciação |
| Alvo estreito | | |

Source: Michael Porter. Competitive advantage: creating and sustaining superior performance. 1989, p. 10.

Also, according to an article by the Tableau tool team (2022), "in practice, you know you have modern *Business Intelligence* when you have a comprehensive view of your organization's data and use that data to generate positive change, eliminate inefficiency and adapt quickly to changes in the market or supply chain". In this way, we can see that we can use BI to achieve certain competitive advantages.

According to the results of the survey carried out by Forbes Insights (2016, pg. 5), *Breakthrough Business Intelligence: How Stronger Governance Becomes A Force* For *Enablement*, significant benefits related to BI were recorded across the spectrum of industries and countries surveyed, as we can see in the image below.

Figure 11: Across the spectrum of industries and countries surveyed, BI offers significant benefits.

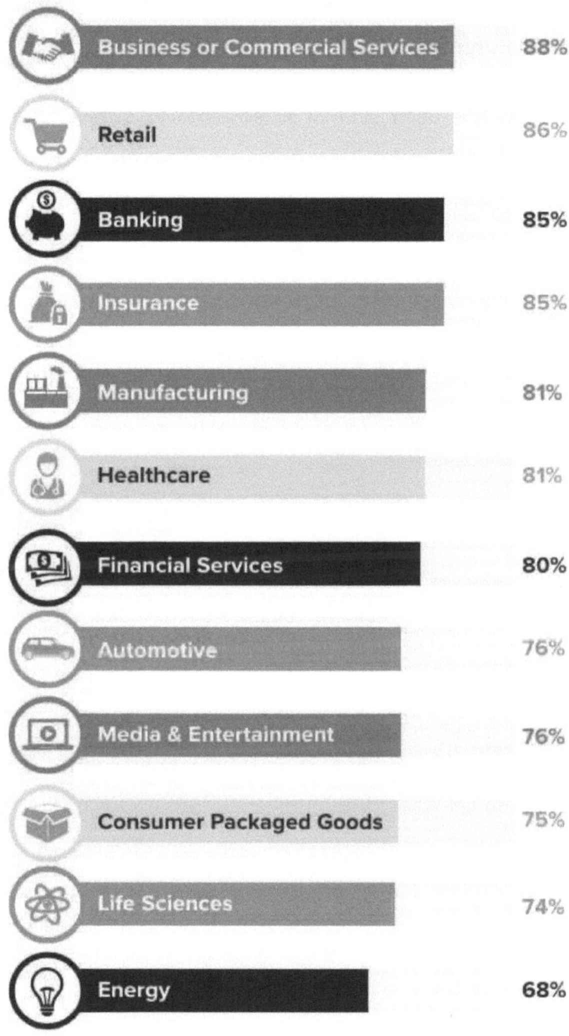


Source: Forbes Insights - 2016, pg. 5

In addition, as seen above, research (FORBES, 2016) has shown that BI has led to positive results in the following areas: consumer metrics, time to market, profitability, employee metrics, revenue, price, product and service mix, logistics and brand evaluation.

Considering what has been said, it is possible to conclude that *Business Intelligence* results in significant benefits for various areas of companies. Consequently, it helps to reduce costs, improve the quality of products and services and allows the company to have closer contact with its consumers. As a result, organizations that adopt *BI* have a greater competitive advantage, as they gain greater control of their results.

# Chapter 8 - Methodology

In this chapter, we will detail the following aspects: how the research was carried out, how the data was collected and what form of research was used in this work.

## 8.1 Type of research

According to Vergara (2016), the classification of a piece of research must take into account the following aspects: "in terms of purpose" and "in terms of means". Thus, with the first aspect described by the author in mind, "in terms of purpose", the study will focus on an explanatory and descriptive investigation, with the aim of demonstrating the main benefit and how BI tools are used in companies.

The second aspect, "in terms of means", is a bibliographical survey, as we have seen in the course of this work, and a field survey carried out by means of a questionnaire. This allowed us to analyze the responses of various professionals in the job market.

## 8.2 Delimitation of the study

As mentioned above, the aim of this study is to understand the main benefit of using *Business Intelligence* tools, as well as how they are used by companies. To this end, studies and research related to the topic have been reported in the various chapters of this book. The survey will be restricted to the responses of 80 professionals working in the market.

## 8.3 Universe and Sample

With the sample universe in mind, the survey will be carried out virtually via a Google Forms link, with the aim of reaching professionals from different age groups who are working in the job market. The sample will therefore be stratified and non-proportional.

## 8.4 Data collection

The data for this study will be collected through bibliographical research and field research. In the first case, data will be collected through books, websites, magazines, newspapers, studies and dissertations that have data related to the subject studied. Next, field research will be carried out in order to answer the problem by means of an online questionnaire.

The questionnaire used in this study was developed with the help of the monograph "A Engenharia da Produção Acadêmica", by the author Manolita Correia Lima. It therefore included closed questions using alternatives. This method makes it possible to obtain more precise data for analysis and understanding. The questionnaire is available in 'Appendix 1 - Survey Model'.

## 8.5 Data processing

With data processing in mind, the data used in the bibliographical research was collected by third parties, either through a study or a survey, and consequently has various types of analysis and conclusions. The data was processed in order to present it in a structured way, allowing for analysis of the various topics covered. In order to show the various results, graphs and tables were used for the reader's better understanding.

## 8.6 Limitations of the Method do

The method chosen for the study has certain limitations, such as: limited scope, given that the questionnaire was applied in Portuguese; the possibility that the sample of people was not representative, but this is a risk that any research carried out over the Internet has .

# Chapter 9 - Research and Analysis of Results

The survey was carried out using the Google Forms platform and was answered by 80 professionals working in the job market. The responses were also collected over a two-week period by sending the survey link via social networks such as *WhatsApp*, *Facebook*, etc.

The questionnaire applied (Appendix 1) was entitled: "Main benefit and use of *Business Intelligence* tools in companies." It had 15 multiple choice questions to be selected by the survey participants.

This chapter presents the results of the fifteen questions asked in the survey. To do this, Microsoft's Power BI tool will be used to process the data, analyze it and develop the tables and graphs that will be used in this chapter.

Question 1: How old are you?

In this question, the participants had six alternatives: under 18; 19 to 25; 26 to 30; 31 to 40; 41 to 50; over 50. Thus, when we analyze the answers we can see that the majority of participants are in the 19 to 25 age group, representing 54 people. In second place are those aged 41 to 50, with 12 responses; followed by third place, ages 31 to 40 with 6; fourth place with ages 26 to 30 with 5 people and, lastly, people over 5, with only 3 responses.

Figure 12: Table counting the number of people who answered the question "How old are you?".

| Alternativas | Contagem |
|---|---|
| 19 a 25 anos | 54 |
| 41 a 50 anos | 12 |
| 31 a 40 anos | 6 |
| 26 a 30 anos | 5 |
| Mais de 50 anos | 3 |
| **Total** | **80** |

Source: Authors, using Power BI.

We can therefore conclude that 67.5% of the people who answered this questionnaire are in the 19 to 25 age group. In second place, those aged 41 to 50 represent 15% of the participants in this survey, as can be seen in the graph below.

Figure 13: Percentage of answers per alternative to the question "How old are you?".

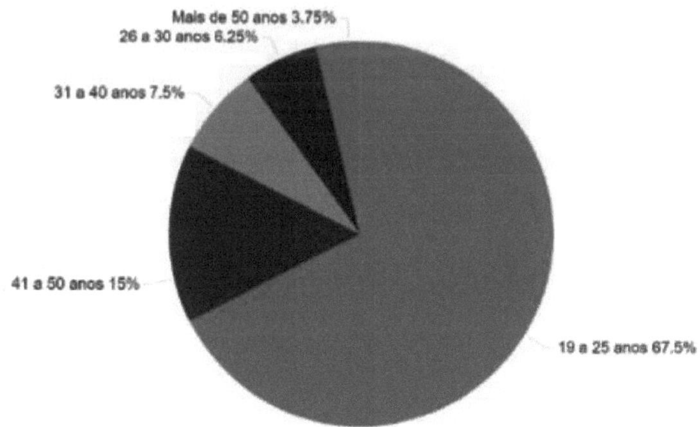


Source: Authors, using Power BI.

Question 2: Which gender do you identify with?

In question two, "Which gender do you identify with?", the participants had five options for answering: Cis Woman (individual who identifies with the biological sex they were born with); Trans Woman (person who was born with a certain biological sex, and does not identify with their body); Cis Man (individual who identifies with the biological sex they were born with); Trans Man (person who was born with a certain biological sex, and does not identify with their body); and other.

Thus, when we analyze the responses, represented both in the table and in the graph developed by the author, we can highlight that most of the people who took part in this survey are cis men, with 42 responses and a representation of 52.5%.

In second place, we can see that 47.5% of people chose the cis women alternative, with 38 responses. We can therefore conclude that the public in this study was divided between these two alternatives, resulting in very close numbers.

Figure 14: Table counting the number of people who answered the question "Which gender do you identify with?".

| Alternativas | Contagem |
|---|---|
| Homem Cis (indivíduo que se identifica com o sexo biológico com o qual nasceu) | 42 |
| Mulher Cis (indivíduo que se identifica com o sexo biológico com o qual nasceu) | 38 |
| **Total** | **80** |

Source: Authors, using Power BI.

Figure 15: Percentage of answers per alternative to the question "Which gender do you identify with?".

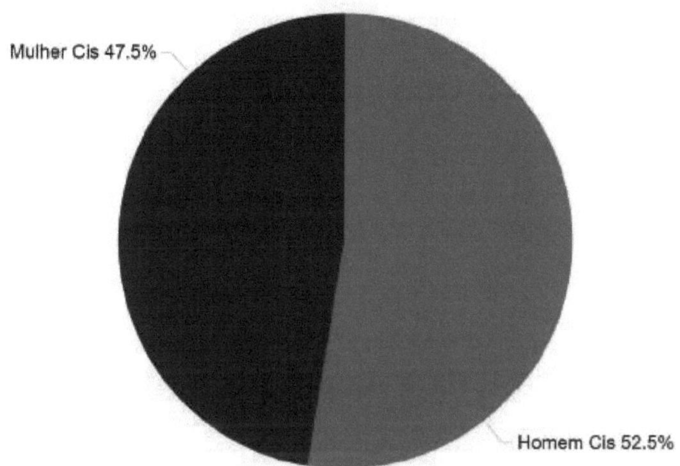


Source: Authors, using Power BI.

Question 3: What level of education do you have?

This question had 7 alternatives: Elementary school; Secondary school; Higher education; Postgraduate studies; Master's degree; Doctorate; and other. Looking at the table and graph below, we can conclude that 73.75% of the participants, with 59 answers, have finished or are still studying at university.

In second place, 10 people are studying for or have completed a postgraduate degree, representing 12.5%. In addition, 7.5% of people, 6 responses, answered High School; 3.75%, 3 responses, chose the alternative Doctorate; and finally, 2.5%, 2 responses, for Master's Degree.

Figure 16: Table counting the number of people who answered the question "What is your schooling?".

| Alternativas | Contagem |
|---|---|
| Ensino Superior | 59 |
| Pós-graduação | 10 |
| Ensino Médio | 6 |
| Doutorado | 3 |
| Mestrado | 2 |
| **Total** | **80** |

Source: Authors, using Power BI.

Figure 17: Percentage of answers per alternative to the question "What is your schooling?".

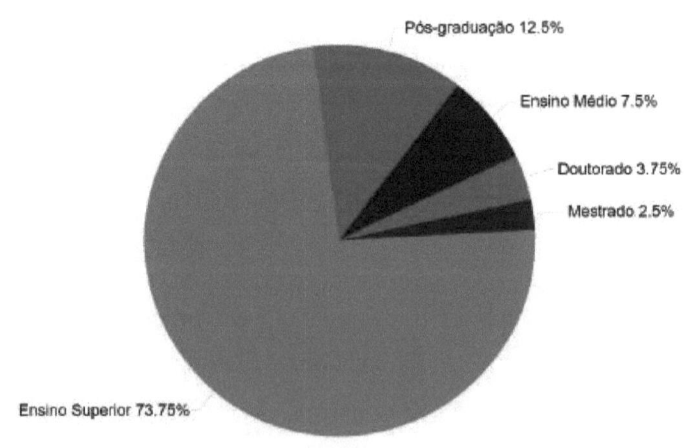


Source: Authors, using Power BI.

Question 4: What is your monthly income?

The answer options for this question were: up to 1 minimum wage; 2 to 4 minimum wages; 5 to 7 minimum wages; and 8 minimum wages or more. In this question, we can see that 52.5% of people earn between 2 and 4 minimum wages; followed by 17 people, 21.25% who earn more than 8 minimum wages.

We can also analyze that 13.75% of the participants earn between 5 and 7 minimum wages. While 10 people, representing 12.5%, have a monthly income of up to 1 minimum wage.

Figure 18: Table counting the number of people who answered the question "What is your monthly income?".

| Alternativas | Contagem |
|---|---|
| De 2 até 4 salários mínimos | 42 |
| De 8 salários mínimos ou mais | 17 |
| De 5 até 7 salários mínimos | 11 |
| Até 1 salário mínimo | 10 |
| **Total** | **80** |

Source: Authors, using Power BI.

Figure 19: Percentage of answers per alternative to the question "What is your monthly income?"

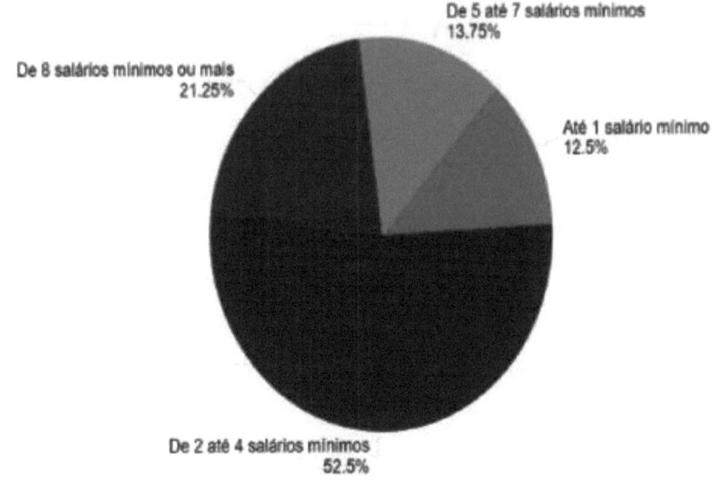


Source: Authors, using Power BI.

Question 5: Which sector of the economy is the company you work for?

The aim of this question was to understand in which sector of the economy the company in which the participants work operates. To this end, the question had 3 alternatives: primary (agriculture, livestock...); secondary (industry); and tertiary (services and commercial activities).

Analyzing the answers, it is possible to conclude that 71.25%, 57 people, currently work in companies in the tertiary sector, i.e. with services and commercial activities. While 28.75%, 23 people, work in companies in the secondary sector, carrying out industrial activities. Finally, none of the participants work in companies in the primary sector (agriculture, livestock, etc.).

Figure 20: Table showing the number of people who answered the question "Which sector of the economy is the company you work for?".

| Alternativas | Contagem |
|---|---|
| Terciário (serviços e atividades comerciais) | 57 |
| Secundário (indústria) | 23 |
| **Total** | **80** |

Source: Authors, using Power BI.

Figure 21: Percentage of answers per alternative to the question "Which sector of the economy is the company you work for?".

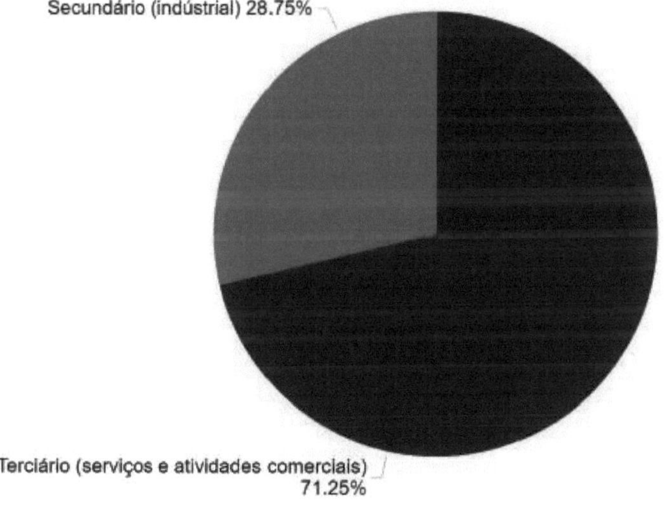


Source: Authors, using Power BI.

Question 6: What area do you work in?

In this question, participants had the following options: Finance; Operations; Marketing and Communication; Sales; Human Resources; Strategic Planning; Information Technology; *Business Intelligence/Analytics*; and other (where it was possible to fill in the field).

It is therefore interesting to highlight the 5 alternatives that received the most responses: Finance, with 26.25% (21 responses); Marketing and Communication, with 20% (16 responses); Sales, with 12.5% (10 responses); *Business Intelligence/Analytics*, with 10% (8 responses); and, finally, Strategic Planning, with 10% (8 responses). It is also possible to analyze all the answers obtained in the survey in the following table and graph.

Figure 22: Table showing the number of people who answered the question "In which area do you work?".

| Alternativas | Contagem |
|---|---|
| Finanças | 21 |
| Marketing e Comunicação | 16 |
| Vendas | 10 |
| Business Intelligence/Analytics | 8 |
| Planejamento Estratégico | 8 |
| Operações | 5 |
| Recursos Humanos | 3 |
| Educação | 2 |
| Jurídico | 2 |
| Assistência técnica | 1 |
| Assuntos Médicos | 1 |
| Customer experience | 1 |
| Gestão | 1 |
| Secretariado | 1 |
| **Total** | **80** |

Source: Authors, using Power BI.

Figure 23: Percentage of answers per alternative to the question "In which area do you work?".

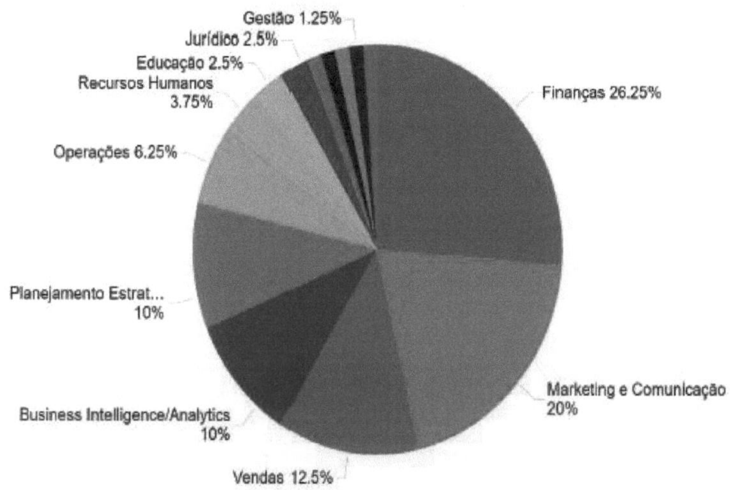


Source: Authors, using Power BI.

Question 7: Are you familiar with the term *Business Intelligence*?

In this case, the participants had only yes or no as alternatives. Thus, when we analyze the answers, we can conclude that the majority of respondents answered that they know the term *Business Intelligence*, representing 85% of people (68 answers). While only 15%, 12 people, chose the alternative that said they don't know the term.

Figure 24: Table showing the number of people who answered the question "Do you know the term *Business Intelligence*?".

| Alternativas | Contagem |
|---|---|
| Sim | 68 |
| Não | 12 |
| **Total** | **80** |

Source: Authors, using Power BI.

Figure 25 Percentage of answers per alternative to the question "Are you familiar with the term *Business Intelligence*?".

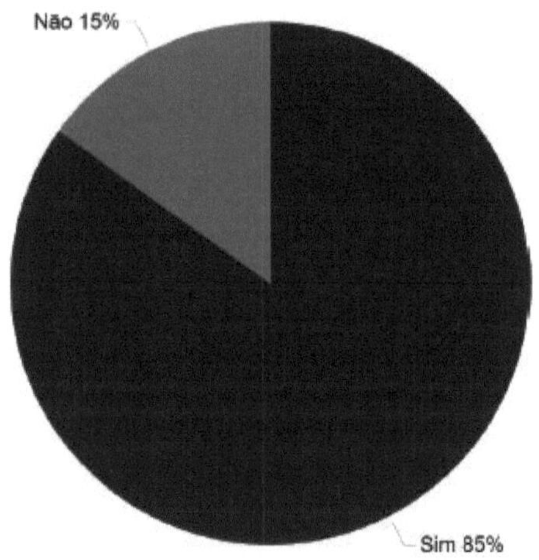


Source: Authors, using Power BI.

Question 8: Does your organization have a Business Intelligence/Analytics department?

For this question, the participants had 3 alternatives: yes, no and I don't know. As a result, 63.75% answered yes (51 people); 20% said that the company does not have the area (16 people); and 16.25% don't know if the area exists in their organization or not (13 people).

Figure 26: Table showing the number of people who answered the question "Does your organization have a *Business Intelligence/Analytics* area?".

| Alternativas | Contagem |
| --- | --- |
| Sim | 51 |
| Não | 16 |
| Não sei | 13 |
| **Total** | **80** |

Source: Authors, using Power BI.

Figure 27: Percentage of answers per alternative to the question "Does your organization have a *Business Intelligence/Analytics* area?".

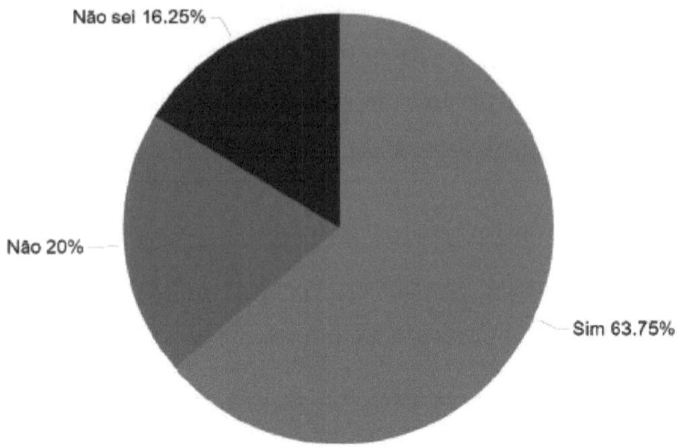


Source: Authors, using Power BI.

Question 9: Does the company you currently work for use any kind of data analysis tool (Power BI, Google Data Studio, Tableau, Qlickview, etc.)?

In view of the topic we are dealing with, this question aims to understand whether organizations are using *Business Intelligence* tools in their day-to-day work. To this end, the question has the following alternatives: yes, no and I don't know; to be chosen by the participants.

Thus, in this question, 68.75% of people (55 responses) answered that the companies they work for have *dashboards* or use some kind of data analysis tool. Meanwhile, 16.25% said that the companies they work for don't use these tools; finally, 15% said they didn't know.

Figure 28: Table counting the number of people who answered the question "Does the company you currently work for use any kind of data analysis tool?"

| Alternativas | Contagem |
|---|---|
| Sim | 55 |
| Não | 13 |
| Não sei | 12 |
| **Total** | **80** |

Source: Authors, using Power BI.

Figure 29: Percentage of answers per alternative to the question "Does the company you currently work for use any kind of data analysis tool?".

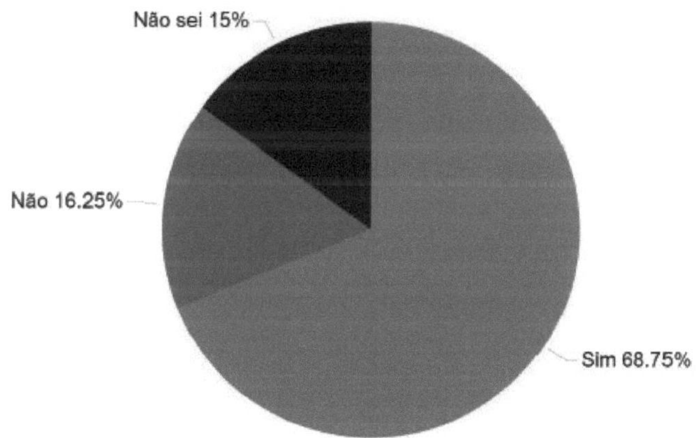


Source: Authors, using Power BI.

Question 10: Which tool does use?

This question is intended to complement the previous question, so the participant can choose between the following BI tools: Power BI, Google

Data Studio, Tableau, Qlikview and another. Participants could also choose more than one alternative in this question.

As a result, we can see that Power BI is the tool most used by companies, accounting for 54.64% of all responses (53). In second and third place were "Not informed" with 26.8% (26) and Tableau with 11.34% (11).

Figure 30: Table showing the number of people who answered the question "Which tool does the company use?".

| Alternativas | Contagem |
|---|---|
| Power Bi | 53 |
| Não Informado | 26 |
| Tableau | 11 |
| Google Data Studio | 4 |
| Qlikview | 3 |
| **Total** | **97** |

Source: Authors, using Power BI.

Figure 31: Percentage of answers per alternative to the question "What tool does the company use?".

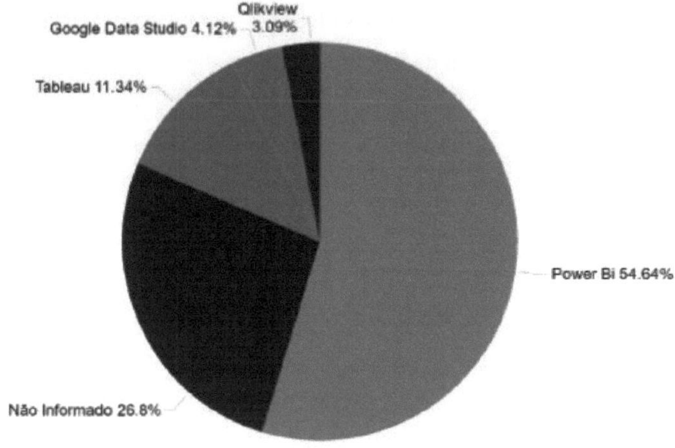


Source: Authors, using Power BI.

Question 11: Does your team/area have a dashboard in any of the tools mentioned in the previous question?

In this question, as "Not informed", we have the survey participants who did not select the tools used by their company, either because they don't know what they are or because they say that the company they work for doesn't use any. Thus, by analyzing the answers, we can conclude that 60% of the areas have some kind of dashboard to help them on a daily basis (48 answers). While only 8.75% of the areas don't have any reports, as we can see in the table and graph below (7 responses).

Figure 2Table showing the number of people who answered the question "Does your team/area have a dashboard in any of the tools mentioned in the previous question?".

| Alternativas | Contagem |
|---|---|
| Sim | 48 |
| Não Informado | 25 |
| Não | 7 |
| **Total** | **80** |

Source: Authors, using Power BI.

Figure 3Percentage of answers per alternative to the question "Does your team/area have a dashboard in any of the tools mentioned in the previous question?".

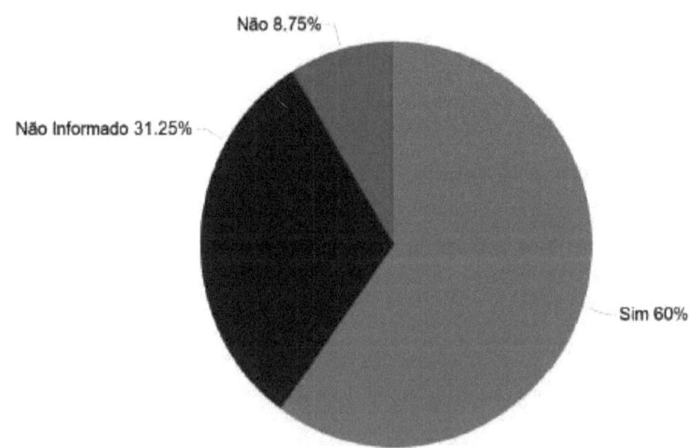


Source: Authors, using Power BI.

Question 12: If the company has reports in any of the tools mentioned above, what are these dashboards used for?

In view of the problem discussed in this study, the main objective of this question is to understand how organizations use these dashboards. To this end, in this question, it was possible to select more than one of the following alternatives: analysis of the organization's results; control of operating expenses; control of people expenses; search for a better relationship with the supplier; search for a better relationship with the consumer; stock control; product price analysis; analysis of the achievement of employee targets; and other functionalities (in which it was possible to fill in the field).

It is therefore interesting to note which alternatives were most chosen by the participants, disregarding those who did not state how they were used. In first place, with 25% of the responses, we have the analysis of the organization's results (45). In second place was the analysis of the achievement of employee targets, with 10.56% (19). Finally, in third place is product price analysis, with 9.44% (17) of the responses. You can also see the other uses in both the table and the graph.

Figure 4Table showing the number of people who answered the question "If the company has reports in any of the tools mentioned above, what are these dashboards used for?".

| Alternativas | Contagem |
|---|---|
| Análise dos resultados da organização | 45 |
| Não Informado | 26 |
| Análise do alcance de metas dos funcionários | 19 |
| Análises de preço de produto | 17 |
| Controle de gastos operacionais | 17 |
| Controle de estoque | 16 |
| Busca por um melhor relacionamento com o consumidor | 15 |
| Busca por um melhor relacionamento com o fornecedor | 11 |
| Controle de gastos com pessoas | 10 |
| Análise de arquivos | 1 |
| Controle de projetos | 1 |
| Todas as opções | 1 |
| Treinamentos dos funcionários | 1 |
| **Total** | **180** |

Source: Authors, using Power BI.

Figure 5Percentage of answers per alternative to the question "If the company has reports in any of the tools mentioned above, what are these dashboards used for?".

| Alternativas | % |
|---|---|
| Análise dos resultados da Organização | 25,00 |
| Não Informado | 14,44 |
| Análise do alcance de metas dos funcionários | 10,56 |
| Análises dos preços dos produtos | 9,44 |
| Controle de gastos operacionais | 9,44 |
| Controle de estoque | 8,89 |
| Busca por melhor relacionamento com o consumidor | 8,33 |
| Busca por melhor relacionamento com o fornecedor | 6,11 |
| Controle de gastos com pessoas | 5,56 |
| Análise de arquivos | 0,55 |
| Controle de projetos | 0,55 |
| Todas as opções | 0,55 |
| Treinamento de funcionários | 0,55 |

Source: Authors, using Power BI.

Question 13: In your opinion, does the use of these dashboards help in the decision-making process, making it more assertive?

In this question, respondents could choose between the following alternatives: yes, no, I don't know. Thus, by analyzing this question, we can conclude that for 90% of the participants, 72 answers, the use of Business Intelligence (BI) tools helps in the decision-making process, making it more assertive. While only 8.75%, 7 answers, stated that they did not agree with the statement.

Figure 6Table showing the number of people who answered the question "In your opinion, does the use of these dashboards help in the decision-making process, making it more assertive?".

| Alternativas | Contagem |
|---|---|
| Sim | 72 |
| Não sei | 7 |
| Não | 1 |
| **Total** | **80** |

Source: Authors, using Power BI.

Figure 7Percentage of answers per alternative to the question "In your opinion, does the use of these dashboards help in the decision-making process, making it more assertive?".

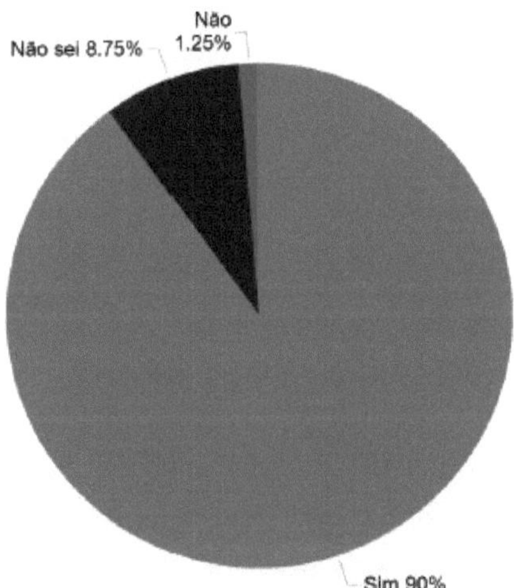


Source: Authors, using Power BI.

Question 14: In your opinion, what is the main benefit of using this type of report?

For this question, participants had the following response options: consolidation of information, allowing the entire company to have the same values in its analysis; greater predictability of the organization's future results and expenses; real-time analysis of the organization's results and expenses; easy access to history; and, finally, other (in which it was possible to fill in the field).

By analyzing the responses, we can deduce that, according to the participants, the main benefit is the consolidation of information, allowing the entire company to have the same values in its analyses, representing 56.25% of the responses (45 responses).

Figure 8In your opinion, what is the main benefit of using this type of report?

| Alternativas | Contagem |
|---|---|
| Consolidação das informações, permitindo que toda a empresa possua os mesmos valores nas suas análises | 45 |
| Análise em tempo real dos resultados e gastos da organização | 16 |
| Maior previsibilidade dos futuros resultados e gastos da organização | 10 |
| Fácil acesso ao histórico | 7 |
| Não sei | 1 |
| Reunir e apresentar os principais KPIs da empresa em todos os níveis ( estratégico, tático e operacional ) permitindo a rápida visualização de desvios em relação à meta e avaliando performance em relação a períodos anteriores | 1 |
| **Total** | **80** |

Source: Authors, using Power BI.

Figure 9Percentage of answers per alternative to the question "In your opinion, what is the main benefit of using this type of report?".

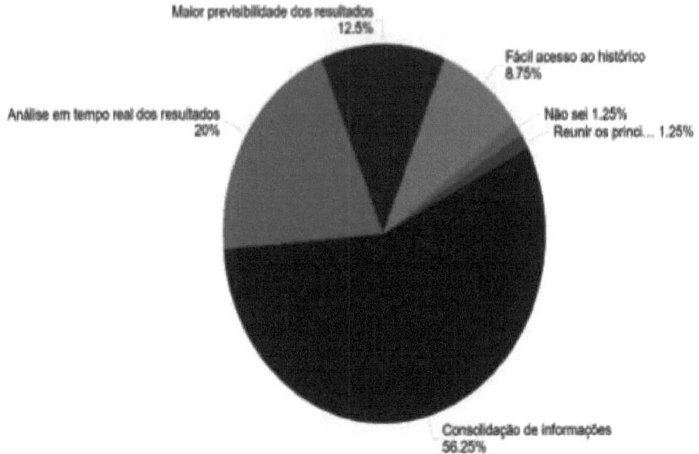


Source: Authors, using Power BI.

Question 15: If your company does not yet use dashboards, would you consider adopting the use of these tools in your area after learning about the benefits of *Business Intelligence*?

Finally, the last question on the questionnaire aimed to find out whether people would consider using these tools in their daily lives. In this case, the answers were: 78.75% of people answered yes (63); 18.75% maybe (15); and only 2.5% (2) chose the alternative that indicated that they would not adopt this type of report.

Figure 10Table with the count of the number of people who answered the question "If your company does not yet use dashboards, would you consider adopting the use of these tools in your area after learning about the benefits of *Business Intelligence*";

| Alternativas | Contagem |
|---|---|
| Sim | 63 |
| Talvez | 15 |
| Não | 2 |
| **Total** | **80** |

Source: Authors, using Power BI.

Figure 11Percentage of answers per alternative to the question "If your company does not yet use dashboards, would you consider adopting the use of these tools in your area after learning about the benefits of *Business Intelligence*?".

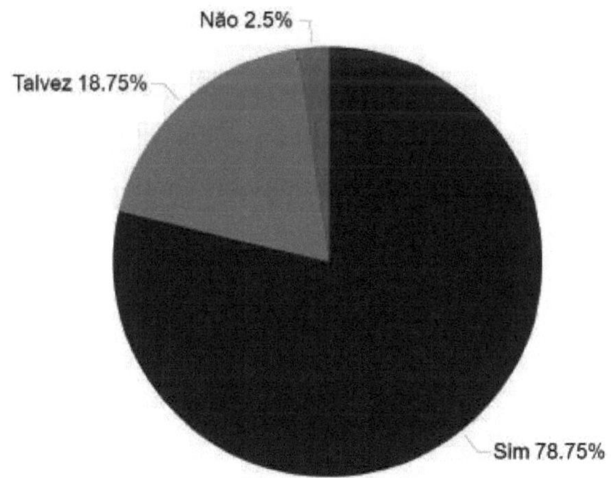


Source: Authors, using Power BI.

## Con concluding remarks

The main objective was to understand the main benefit of *Business Intelligence* tools for companies. It also aimed to verify the ways in which these tools are being used by companies. Finally, the aim was to demonstrate the importance of using these tools and the advantages they offer.

A number of subjects involving the topic of Business Intelligence were addressed. To this end, extensive bibliographical research was carried out, covering subjects such as: the importance of Business Intelligence and Data Analysis; an introduction to the methods and tools used by BI, with a focus on Power BI; Strategic Management; the decision-making process; and competitive advantage.

In this way, the various chapters introduce the topic to the reader, showing what it is and what the main benefits of Business Intelligence are in the day-to-day running of an organization. As we saw earlier, it is very important for a company to know itself and have control of its data, so that it can grow more and more.

Another part of this work was a field survey of 80 professionals in the job market. The aim was to find out the main benefit and how *Business Intelligence* tools, such as Power Bi, are used in companies.

Thus, as we saw in ' Chapter 9 - Research and Analysis of Results', the study showed that 56.25% of the participants, 45 people, answered that the main benefit of using *Business Intelligence* tools is the consolidation of information, allowing the whole company to have the same values in their analysis.

In addition, when we talk about the usability of the tools in organizations, we can highlight the two alternatives that obtained the most responses in the survey: in first place, with 25%, the use focused on analyzing the results of the organization; and in second place, with 10.56%, we have the use focused on analyzing the achievement of employee goals.

The last question in the survey was aimed at understanding whether people, after learning about the benefits of *Business Intelligence,* would consider adopting the use of these tools in their areas. For this question, 78.75% of the participants answered yes, showing that most of those interviewed would consider including these tools in their daily lives.

In conclusion, it is possible to understand that the advent of the digital age has resulted in a wide availability of different types of data, making the use of these tools increasingly essential for organizations. As we saw in the literature survey and the field research, most companies recognize the importance and benefits of *Business Intelligence*, and are adopting the use of BI tools and creating departments to do so.

## Bibliography:


2022 Gartner® Magic Quadrant$^{tm}$ I Microsoft Power BI. Available at: <https://info.microsoft.com/ww-landing-2022-gartner-mq-report-on-bi-and-analytics-platforms.html?lcid=en-us>. Accessed on: July 5, 2022.

Abdala, Márcio M. Administração Estratégica. Available at: My Library, GEN Group, 2019.

ACCENTURE. From productivity to outcomes: using the internet of things to drive future business strategies. 2015, p. 8.

ANSOFF, H. I. Implementing Strategic Management. 2 ed. São Paulo: Atlas, 1993

BALTZAN, Palge. Management-oriented technology. Porto Alegre: AMGH, 2016.

BATEMAN, T. S. and SNELL. S. A. Management: Building competitive advantage. São Paulo: Atlas, 1998.

BRAGHITTONI, R. Business Intelligence: Implementing the Right Way at Zero Cost. São Paulo/SP: Editora Casa do Código, 2017, pg. 28.

CANARY, V.P. Decision Making in the Context of Big Data. 74f. Monograph Department of Administrative Sciences, Federal University of Rio Grande do Sul, 2013.

CERTO, S. C. Administração estratégica: planejamento e implementação da estratégia. São Paulo: Makron Books, 1993.

Chen, H., Chiang, R. H., & Storey, V. C. (2012). Business intelligence and analytics: From big data to big impact. MIS Quarterly, 36(4), 1165-1188 .

CRUZ, E.P.; COVA, C.J. G. Teoria das Decisões: Um Estudo do Método Lexicográfico RPCA, Rio de Janeiro, v. 1, n. 1, p. 26-35, set./dez. 2007.

DAILEY, Doug. The enterprise data warehouse of the future. Available at: <https://www.ibm.com/blogs/journey-to-ai/2019/03/the-enterprise-data-warehouse-of-the-future/>. Accessed on: July 5, 2022.

DINO. Data analysis drives increase in revenues, says study. Available at: <https://www.terra.com.br/noticias/analise-de-dados-impulsiona-aumento-nas-receitas-diz-estudo,70976912c1a1805b72600468cb546938v506s47t.html>. June 26, 2022.

EXAME. We have more data than ever. How can we use it to our advantage? Available at: <https://exame.com/carreira/dados-uso-favor/>. Accessed on: June 24, 2022.

FERNANDES, Bruno Henrique R.; BERTON, Luiz H. Administração estratégica: Da competência empreendedora à avaliação de desempenho - 2ª Edição. [Type the Place of the Publisher]: Editora Saraiva, 2017. Available at: https://integrada.minhabiblioteca.com.br/#/books/9788502146013/. Accessed on: June 4, 2022.

GOOGLE. Get to know Data Studio. Available at: <https://support.google.com/datastudio/answer/6283323?hl=pt-BR>. Accessed on: June 26, 2022.

HARVARD. The evolution of decision making: How leading organizations are developing a data-driven culture. Harvard business review, 20 Apr 2016. Available at: <https://hbr.org/sponsored/2016/04/the-evolution-of-decision-making-how-leading-organizations-are-developing-a-data-driven-culture>. Accessed on: June 26, 2022.

IDC. IDC FutureScape: Worldwide Data, Integration, and Analytics 2020 Predictions. Available at: <https://www.oracle.com/br/a/ocom/docs/solutions/business-analytics/idc-futurescape-2020-predictions.pdf>. Accessed on July 7, 2022.

IDC. Data creation and replication will grow at a faster rate than installed storage capacity, according to the IDC global DataSphere and StorageSphere forecasts. Available at: <https://www.idc.com/getdoc.jsp?containerId=prUS47560321>. Accessed on: June 24, 2022

INFORMS. Analytics Society. Available at: <https://connect.informs.org/analytics/home>. Accessed on: May 26, 2022.

INFORMS. What are Operations Research and Analytics? Available at: <https://www.informs.org/Explore/Operations-Research-Analytics>. Accessed on September 18, 2022.

INSIGHTS, Forbes. BREAKTHROUGH BUSINESS INTELLIGENCE. Available at: <https://images.forbes.com/forbesinsights/qlik_bi/BreakthroughBusinessIntelligence.pdf>. Accessed on: June 26, 2022.

LIMA, Manolita Correia. Monografia: A Engenharia da Produção Acadêmica. 2 ª ed. São Paulo: Saraiva, 2010.

LU, Mengwei. Discovering Microsoft Self-service BI solution: Power BI. 2014. Haaga-Helia - Univesity of Applied Sciences.

Maçães, Manuel Alberto R. Planning, Strategy and Decision Making - Vol IV. Available at: My Library, Almedina Group (Portugal), 2018.011.

MAGRANI, Eduardo. The internet of things. Editora FGV, 2018, pg. 44 - 77.

MARTINS, Alvaro Horowicz. The use of computerized systems for better management of aviation companies. 2016.

MICROSOFT. Microsoft Power BI interactive learning. Microsoft, 2018. Available at: <https://docs.microsoft.com/pt-br/power-bi/guidedlearning/gettingstarted#step-1>. Accessed on: 25 Feb. 2018.

MICROSOFT. What is Power BI? Available at: <https://docs.microsoft.com/pt-br/power-bi/fundamentals/power-bi-overview>. Accessed on: June 26, 2022.

NETO, F. P.de F. TCC: Business Intelligence Applied to Support Decision-Making in Public Security, 2014. Available at: <https://ppgcc.ufersa.edu.br/wpcontent/uploads/sites/42/2014/09/francisco-paula-de-freitas-neto.pdf>.

Neto, Jocildo Figueiredo, C. and Erico Veras Marques. Making management decisions with data analytics. Available at: My Library, Editora Alta Books, 2020.

OHMAE, K. The mind of strategist. Harmondsworth, Peguin Books, 1983.

OLIVEIRA, Djalma de Pinho Rebouças D. Administração estratégica na prática: a competitividade para administrar o futuro das empresas, 8th edition. GEN Group, 2013. Available at: https://integrada.minhabiblioteca.com.br/#/books/9788522475612/. Accessed on: June 5, 2022.

OLIVEIRA, Djalma de Pinho Rebouças D. Estratégia empresarial: uma abordagem empreendedora. 2ed. São Paulo: Atlas, 1991

PORTER, Michael E. Competitive advantage: creating and sustaining superior performance. Rio de Janeiro: Editora Elsevier, 1989 - 37th Reprint.

PRIMAK, Fábio Vinicius da Silva. Decisions with B.I. (Business Intelligence). Rio de Janeiro: Editora Ciência Moderna, 2008.

BD2 WAREHOUSE PROJECT. ETL for OLAP. Available at: < *https://sites.google.com/site/proyectoalmacenbd2/home/etl-para-la-olap>*. Accessed on: 04 May 2022

PURDY, Mark; davarzani, Ladan; ovanessoff, Armen. How the internet of things can lead to the next wave of growth in Brazil. Harvard Business Review Brazil, Nov. 2015.

QLIKVIEW. Advanced and interactive analysis and dashboards. Available at: <https://www.qlik.com/pt-br/products/qlikview>. Accessed on: June 26, 2022.

SHARDA, Ramesh. Business Intelligence and Data Analysis for Business Management. Available at: My Library, (4th edition). Group A, 2019.

TABLEAU. What is business intelligence? Your guide to BI and why it's important. Available at: https://www.tableau.com/pt-br/learn/articles/business-intelligence. Accessed on November 08, 2022.

TABLEAU. What is Tableau? Available at: <https://www.tableau.com/pt-br/why-tableau/what-is-tableau>. Accessed on: June 26, 2022.

TZU, Sun. The art of war. Editora Schwarcz-Companhia das Letras, 2019.

VERGARA, Sylvia Constant. 16th ed. Research Projects and Reports in Administration. São Paulo: Atlas, 2016

VIANNA, W. B.; DUTRA, M. L. Big Data and Information Management: Modeling the Decision Context Supported by Systemography. Revista Informação e Informação, Londrina, v. 21, n. 1, p. 185 - 212, jan./abr. 2016.

W. Eckerson, Smart Companies in the 21st Century: The Secrets of Creating Successful Business Intelligent Solutions. The Data Warehousing Institute, Seattle, WA, 2003, p. 32, Illustration 5.

WHITTINGTON, R. What is strategy? Thomson, 2004

# Annexes

## Annex 1 - Survey template

Dear participant, the following survey aims to understand what the main benefit is and how Business Intelligence tools are used in companies. The questionnaire is completely anonymous, so at no point will the participant be identified.

1) How old are you?

a) Under 18.
b) 19 to 25 years old.
c) 26 to 30 years old.
d) 31 to 40 years old.
e) 41 to 50 years old.
f) Over 50 years old.

2) Which gender do you identify with?

a) Cis woman (individual who identifies with the biological sex they were born with).
b) Trans woman (a person who was born with a certain biological sex and does not identify with her body).
c) Cis man (an individual who identifies with the biological sex they were born with).
d) Trans man (a person who was born with a certain biological sex and does not identify with their body).
e) Other.

3) What is your schooling?

a) Elementary school.
b) High school.
c) Higher education.
d) Postgraduate studies.
e) Master's degree.
f) PhD.
g) Other.

4) What is your monthly income?
    a) Up to 1 minimum wage.
    b) From 2 to 4 minimum wages.
    c) From 5 to 7 minimum wages.
    d) 8 minimum wages or more.

5) Which sector of the economy is the company you work for?
    a) Primary (agriculture, livestock...).
    b) Secondary (industry).
    c) Tertiary (services and commercial activities).

6) What area do you work in?
    a) Finance.
    b) Operations.
    c) Marketing and Communication.
    d) Sales.
    e) Human Resources.
    f) Strategic Planning.
    g) Information Technology.
    h) Business Intelligence/Analytics.
    i) Other.

7) Are you familiar with the term *Business Intelligence*?
    a) Yes.
    b) No.

8) Does your organization have a *Business Intelligence/Analytics* department?
    a) Yes.
    b) No
    c) I don't know

9) Does the company you work for currently use any kind of data analysis tool (Power BI, Google Data Studio, Tableau, Qlickview, etc.)?
    a) Yes.
    b) No.

c) I don't know.

10) What tool does the company use?

a) Power Bi.
b) Google Data Studio.
c) Tableau.
d) Qlikview.
e) Other.

11) Does your team/area have a *dashboard* in any of the tools mentioned in the previous question?

a) Yes.
b) No.

12) If the company has reports in any of the tools mentioned above, what are these *dashboards* used for?

a) Analysis of the organization's results.
b) Control of operating costs.
c) Control of personnel costs.
d) Search for a better relationship with the supplier.
e) Search for a better relationship with the consumer.
f) Stock control.
g) Product price analysis.
h) Analysis of the achievement of employee targets.
i) Other.

13) In your opinion, does the use of these *dashboards* help in the decision-making process, making it more assertive?

a) Yes.
b) No.
c) I don't know.

14) In your opinion, what is the main benefit of using this type of report?

a) Consolidation of information, allowing the entire company to have the same values in its analysis.

b) Greater predictability of the organization's future results and expenses.

c) Real-time analysis of the organization's results and expenses.

d) Easy access to history.

e) Another .

15) If your company doesn't already use *dashboards*, would you consider adopting the use of these tools in your area after learning about the benefits of *Business Intelligence*?

a) Yes.

b) No.

c) Maybe.

Annex 2 - List of Figures

Printed by Books on Demand GmbH, Norderstedt / Germany